Trampoline

GYMNASTICS
GOALBOOK

© Dream Co Publishing 2020. ISBN 978-0-9951317-3-6

Sports club bulk orders: orders@dreamcomedia.nz

Image credit: Valeriya Novozhonova/Eugene Onischenko/Shutterstock.com

Contents:

Info	page 1
Encouraging quotes	page 2
Yearly Training Goals	page 4
Training Goals	page 8
Competition Goals	page 64

Gymnastics Info:

Name: _____

Age: _____

Level: _____

Club: _____

Coach/es: _____

Favourite skill/s: _____

_____

Favourite trampoline event/s: _____

_____

Favourite Olympic gymnast: _____

_____

Favourite leotard colour: _____

Inspirational words or quotes:

Inspirational words or quotes:

My Yearly Training Goals:

Date: _____

_____

_____

_____

_____

_____

_____

_____

_____

_____

_____

_____

_____

_____

_____

 You can do it!

My Yearly Training Outcomes:

Date: _____

_____

_____

_____

_____

_____

_____

_____

_____

_____

_____

_____

_____

_____

_____

♡ *Go for gold!* ♡

My Yearly Training Goals:

Date: _____

_____

_____

_____

_____

_____

_____

_____

_____

_____

_____

_____

_____

_____

_____

_____

_____

♡ Dreams are possible. ♡

My Yearly Training Outcomes:

Date: _____

_____
_____
_____
_____
_____
_____
_____
_____
_____
_____
_____
_____
_____
_____
_____
_____

♡ *Flipping out is fun!* ♡

My Training Goals:

Date: _____

_____
_____
_____
_____
_____
_____
_____
_____
_____
_____
_____
_____
_____
_____
_____

 Don't give up!

My Training Outcomes:

Date: _____

_____

_____

_____

_____

_____

_____

_____

_____

_____

_____

_____

_____

_____

_____

 Train like a champion.

My Training Goals:

Date: _____

_____
_____
_____
_____
_____
_____
_____
_____
_____
_____
_____
_____
_____
_____
_____
_____
_____
_____

 Aim high!

My Training Outcomes:

Date: _____

_____

_____

_____

_____

_____

_____

_____

_____

_____

_____

_____

_____

_____

_____

_____

_____

 You're a star!

My Training Goals:

Date: _____

_____
_____
_____
_____
_____
_____
_____
_____
_____
_____
_____
_____
_____
_____
_____

 If you don't try -- you won't know what you're actually capable of.

My Training Outcomes:

Date: _____

_____
_____
_____
_____
_____
_____
_____
_____
_____
_____
_____
_____
_____
_____
_____
_____
_____

 You got this!

My Training Goals:

Date: _____

 You're amazing.

My Training Outcomes:

Date: _____

_____
_____
_____
_____
_____
_____
_____
_____
_____
_____
_____
_____
_____
_____
_____
_____

♡ *Believe – achieve.* ♡

My Training Goals:

Date: _____

_____
_____
_____
_____
_____
_____
_____
_____
_____
_____
_____
_____
_____
_____
_____
_____
_____

♡ ...it's a gymnast thing. ♡

My Training Outcomes:

Date: _____

_____

_____

_____

_____

_____

_____

_____

_____

_____

_____

_____

_____

_____

_____

_____

_____

 Be flexible, be strong. And smile!

My Training Goals:

Date: _____

_____
_____
_____
_____
_____
_____
_____
_____
_____
_____
_____
_____
_____
_____
_____
_____

 You can do it!

My Training Outcomes:

Date: _____

_____
_____
_____
_____
_____
_____
_____
_____
_____
_____
_____
_____
_____
_____
_____
_____

Go for gold!

My Training Goals:

Date: _____

 Dreams are possible.

My Training Outcomes:

Date: _____

_____
_____
_____
_____
_____
_____
_____
_____
_____
_____
_____
_____
_____
_____
_____

♡ *Flipping out is fun!* ♡

My Training Goals:

Date: _____

Don't give up!

My Training Outcomes:

Date: _____

_____
_____
_____
_____
_____
_____
_____
_____
_____
_____
_____
_____
_____
_____
_____
_____

♡ *Train like a champion.* ♡

My Training Goals:

Date: _____

_____

_____

_____

_____

_____

_____

_____

_____

_____

_____

_____

_____

_____

_____

_____

Aim high!

My Training Outcomes:

Date: _____

You're a star!

My Training Goals:

Date: _____

 Trampolining counts as flying.

My Training Outcomes:

Date: _____

 I love gymnastics!

My Training Goals:

Date: _____

_____

_____

_____

_____

_____

_____

_____

_____

_____

_____

_____

_____

_____

_____

_____

 If you don't try – you won't know what you're actually capable of.

My Training Outcomes:

Date: _____

You got this!

My Training Goals:

Date: _____

_____
_____
_____
_____
_____
_____
_____
_____
_____
_____
_____
_____
_____
_____
_____
_____

Trampolining is the best!

My Training Outcomes:

Date: _____

___

Don't forget to have fun.

My Training Goals:

Date: _____

 Run towards a challenge, not away from it.

My Training Outcomes:

Date: _____

_____
_____
_____
_____
_____
_____
_____
_____
_____
_____
_____
_____
_____
_____
_____
_____

Fly like an eagle.

My Training Goals:

Date: _____

_____
_____
_____
_____
_____
_____
_____
_____
_____
_____
_____
_____
_____
_____
_____

 You're amazing.

My Training Outcomes:

Date: _____

_____

_____

_____

_____

_____

_____

_____

_____

_____

_____

_____

_____

_____

_____

Believe – achieve.

My Training Goals:

Date: _____

_____
_____
_____
_____
_____
_____
_____
_____
_____
_____
_____
_____
_____
_____
_____
_____

...it's a gymnast thing.

My Training Outcomes:

Date: _____

_____

_____

_____

_____

_____

_____

_____

_____

_____

_____

_____

_____

_____

_____

_____

_____

Be flexible, be strong. And smile!

My Training Goals:

Date: _____

 You can do it!

My Training Outcomes:

Date: _____

Go for gold!

My Training Goals:

Date: _____

 Dreams are possible.

My Training Outcomes:

Date: _____

_____
_____
_____
_____
_____
_____
_____
_____
_____
_____
_____
_____
_____
_____
_____
_____

 Flipping out is fun!

My Training Goals:

Date: _____

_____

_____

_____

_____

_____

_____

_____

_____

_____

_____

_____

_____

_____

_____

_____

_____

♡ *Don't give up!* ♡

My Training Outcomes:

Date: _____

_____

_____

_____

_____

_____

_____

_____

_____

_____

_____

_____

_____

_____

_____

 Train like a champion.

My Training Goals:

Date: _____

_____
_____
_____
_____
_____
_____
_____
_____
_____
_____
_____
_____
_____
_____
_____
_____

♡ *Aim high!* ♡

My Training Outcomes:

Date: _____

_____
_____
_____
_____
_____
_____
_____
_____
_____
_____
_____
_____
_____
_____
_____

You're a star!

My Training Goals:

Date: _____

_____
_____
_____
_____
_____
_____
_____
_____
_____
_____
_____
_____
_____
_____
_____

Trampolining counts as flying.

My Training Outcomes:

Date: _____

_____
_____
_____
_____
_____
_____
_____
_____
_____
_____
_____
_____
_____
_____
_____
_____
_____

♡ I love trampolining! ♡

My Training Goals:

Date: _____

_____

_____

_____

_____

_____

_____

_____

_____

_____

_____

_____

_____

_____

_____

_____

 If you don't try – you won't know what you're actually capable of.

My Training Outcomes:

Date: _____

You got this!

My Training Goals:

Date: _____

_____

_____

_____

_____

_____

_____

_____

_____

_____

_____

_____

_____

_____

_____

_____

_____

Trampolining is the best!

My Training Outcomes:

Date: _____

 Don't forget to have fun.

My Training Goals:

Date: _____

 Run towards a challenge, not away from it.

My Training Outcomes:

Date: _____

Trampolining counts as flying.

My Training Goals:

Date: _____

_____
_____
_____
_____
_____
_____
_____
_____
_____
_____
_____
_____
_____
_____
_____
_____

♡ *You're amazing.* ♡

My Training Outcomes:

Date: _____

Believe – achieve.

My Training Goals:

Date: _____

...it's a gymnast thing.

My Training Outcomes:

Date: _____

Be flexible, be strong. And smile!

My Training Goals:

Date: _____

_____
_____
_____
_____
_____
_____
_____
_____
_____
_____
_____
_____
_____
_____
_____

 You can do it!

My Training Outcomes:

Date: _____

_____

_____

_____

_____

_____

_____

_____

_____

_____

_____

_____

_____

_____

_____

_____

_____

Go for gold!

My Training Goals:

Date: _____

_____

_____

_____

_____

_____

_____

_____

_____

_____

_____

_____

_____

_____

_____

_____

 Dreams are possible.

My Training Outcomes:

Date: _____

 Flipping out is fun!

My Training Goals:

Date: _____

___

Don't give up!

My Training Outcomes:

Date: _____

_____
_____
_____
_____
_____
_____
_____
_____
_____
_____
_____
_____
_____
_____
_____

 Train like a champion.

My Competition Goals:

Date: _____

Competition name: _____

_____

_____

_____

_____

_____

_____

_____

_____

_____

_____

_____

_____

COMMENTS: _____

_____

 Trampolining counts as flying.

My Competition Achievements:

Date: _____

Competition name: _____

_____

_____

_____

_____

_____

_____

_____

_____

_____

_____

_____

_____

_____

SCORES: _____

_____

♡ I love gymnastics! ♡

My Competition Goals:

Date: _____

Competition name: _____

_____
_____
_____
_____
_____
_____
_____
_____
_____
_____
_____
_____

COMMENTS: _____
_____

If you don't try – you won't know what you're actually capable of.

My Competition Achievements:

Date: _____

Competition name: _____

_____

_____

_____

_____

_____

_____

_____

_____

_____

_____

_____

SCORES: _____

_____

♡ *You got this!* ♡

My Competition Goals:

Date: _____

Competition name: _____

_____

_____

_____

_____

_____

_____

_____

_____

_____

_____

_____

_____

COMMENTS: _____

_____

Trampolining is the best!

My Competition Achievements:

Date: _____

Competition name: _____

_____

_____

_____

_____

_____

_____

_____

_____

_____

_____

_____

_____

SCORES: _____

_____

 Don't forget to have fun.

My Competition Goals:

Date: _____

Competition name: _____

_____
_____
_____
_____
_____
_____
_____
_____
_____
_____
_____
_____

COMMENTS: _____

_____

 Run towards a challenge, not away from it.

My Competition Achievements:

Date: _____

Competition name: _____

_____

_____

_____

_____

_____

_____

_____

_____

_____

_____

_____

_____

_____

SCORES: _____

_____

 Fly like an eagle.

My Competition Goals:

Date: _____

Competition name: _____

_____

_____

_____

_____

_____

_____

_____

_____

_____

_____

_____

_____

COMMENTS: _____

_____

♡ *You're amazing.* ♡

My Competition Achievements:

Date: _____

Competition name: _____

_____

_____

_____

_____

_____

_____

_____

_____

_____

_____

_____

_____

SCORES: _____

_____

♡ Believe – achieve. ♡

My Competition Goals:

Date: _____

Competition name: _____

_____
_____
_____
_____
_____
_____
_____
_____
_____
_____
_____
_____
_____

COMMENTS: _____
_____

...it's a gymnast thing.

My Competition Achievements:

Date: _____

Competition name: _____

_____

_____

_____

_____

_____

_____

_____

_____

_____

_____

_____

_____

_____

SCORES: _____

_____

♡ *Be flexible, be strong. And smile!* ♡

My Competition Goals:

Date: _____

Competition name: _____

_____

_____

_____

_____

_____

_____

_____

_____

_____

_____

_____

_____

_____

COMMENTS: _____

_____

 You can do it!

My Competition Achievements:

Date: _____

Competition name: _____

_____
_____
_____
_____
_____
_____
_____
_____
_____
_____
_____
_____

SCORES: _____
_____

♡ *Go for gold!* ♡

My Competition Goals:

Date: _____

Competition name: _____

_____
_____
_____
_____
_____
_____
_____
_____
_____
_____
_____
_____
_____

COMMENTS: _____

_____

 Dreams are possible.

My Competition Achievements:

Date: _____

Competition name: _____

_____

_____

_____

_____

_____

_____

_____

_____

_____

_____

_____

SCORES: _____

_____

Flipping out is fun!

My Competition Goals:

Date: _____

Competition name: _____

_____

_____

_____

_____

_____

_____

_____

_____

_____

_____

_____

COMMENTS: _____

_____

Don't give up!

My Competition Achievements:

Date: _____

Competition name: _____

_____

_____

_____

_____

_____

_____

_____

_____

_____

_____

_____

_____

SCORES: _____

_____

♡ *Train like a champion.* ♡

My Competition Goals:

Date: _____

Competition name: _____

_____
_____
_____
_____
_____
_____
_____
_____
_____
_____
_____
_____
_____

COMMENTS: _____

_____

♡ Aim high! ♡

My Competition Achievements:

Date: _____

Competition name: _____

_____

_____

_____

_____

_____

_____

_____

_____

_____

_____

_____

_____

_____

SCORES: _____

_____

 You're a star!

My Competition Goals:

Date: _____

Competition name: _____

_____

_____

_____

_____

_____

_____

_____

_____

_____

_____

_____

_____

COMMENTS: _____

_____

Trampolining counts as flying.

My Competition Achievements:

Date: _____

Competition name: _____

_____

_____

_____

_____

_____

_____

_____

_____

_____

_____

_____

_____

SCORES: _____

_____

 I love trampolining!

My Competition Goals:

Date: _____

Competition name: _____

_____
_____
_____
_____
_____
_____
_____
_____
_____
_____
_____
_____

COMMENTS: _____
_____

 If you don't try – you won't know what you're actually capable of.

My Competition Achievements:

Date: _____

Competition name: _____

_____

_____

_____

_____

_____

_____

_____

_____

_____

_____

_____

SCORES: _____

_____

 You got this!

My Competition Goals:

Date: _____

Competition name: _____

_____

_____

_____

_____

_____

_____

_____

_____

_____

_____

_____

_____

COMMENTS: _____

_____

♡ *Aim high!* ♡

My Competition Achievements:

Date: _____

Competition name: _____

_____
_____
_____
_____
_____
_____
_____
_____
_____
_____
_____
_____

SCORES: _____
_____

 You're a star!

My Competition Goals:

Date: _____

Competition name: _____

_____

_____

_____

_____

_____

_____

_____

_____

_____

_____

_____

_____

_____

COMMENTS: _____

_____

Trampolining counts as flying.

My Competition Achievements:

Date: _____

Competition name: _____

_____

_____

_____

_____

_____

_____

_____

_____

_____

_____

_____

SCORES: _____

_____

 I love gymnastics!

My Competition Goals:

Date: _____

Competition name: _____

_____

_____

_____

_____

_____

_____

_____

_____

_____

_____

_____

_____

COMMENTS: _____

_____

 Trampolining is the best!

My Competition Achievements:

Date: _____

Competition name: _____

_____

_____

_____

_____

_____

_____

_____

_____

_____

_____

_____

SCORES: _____

_____

 Don't forget to have fun.

My Competition Goals:

Date: _____

Competition name: _____

_____

_____

_____

_____

_____

_____

_____

_____

_____

_____

_____

_____

COMMENTS: _____

_____

♡ *Run towards a challenge, not away from it.* ♡

My Competition Achievements:

Date: _____

Competition name: _____

_____

_____

_____

_____

_____

_____

_____

_____

_____

_____

_____

_____

SCORES: _____

_____

Fly like an eagle.

Extra notes

www.ingramcontent.com/pod-product-compliance
Lightning Source LLC
Chambersburg PA
CBHW070759020526
44118CB00036B/2069